Smiles for Baby

Written and Illustrated by
Joshveena Thirukonda Jholl

Smiles for Baby

Written and illustrated by Joshveena Thirukonda Jholl

Copyright © 2023 Jhollygoodtimes

All rights reserved. No part of this book may be reproduced without written permission from the publisher.

First printed in December 2023

Published by Jhollygoodtimes
www.jhollygoodtimes.com

ISBN 978-0-6486142-0-3

This book belongs to

_____

Hello baby, what will you see?
Someone smiling, who could it be?
Let's turn the page to find out who…

It's **mummy** smiling at you!

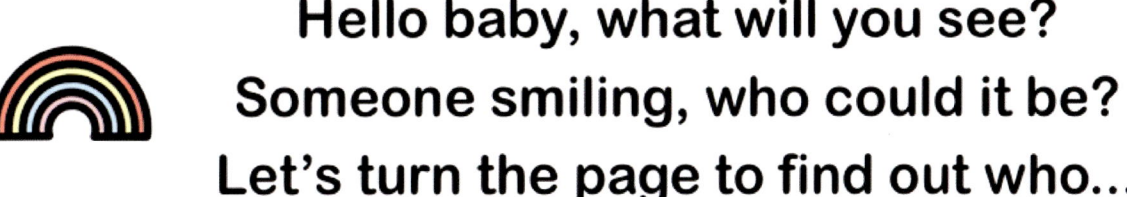
Hello baby, what will you see?
Someone smiling, who could it be?
Let's turn the page to find out who…

It's **daddy** smiling at you!

Hello baby, what will you see?
Someone smiling, who could it be?
Let's turn the page to find out who…

It's **sister** smiling at you!

Hello baby, what will you see?
Someone smiling, who could it be?
Let's turn the page to find out who…

It's **brother** smiling at you!

Hello baby, what will you see?
Someone smiling, who could it be?
Let's turn the page to find out who…

It's **grandma** smiling at you!

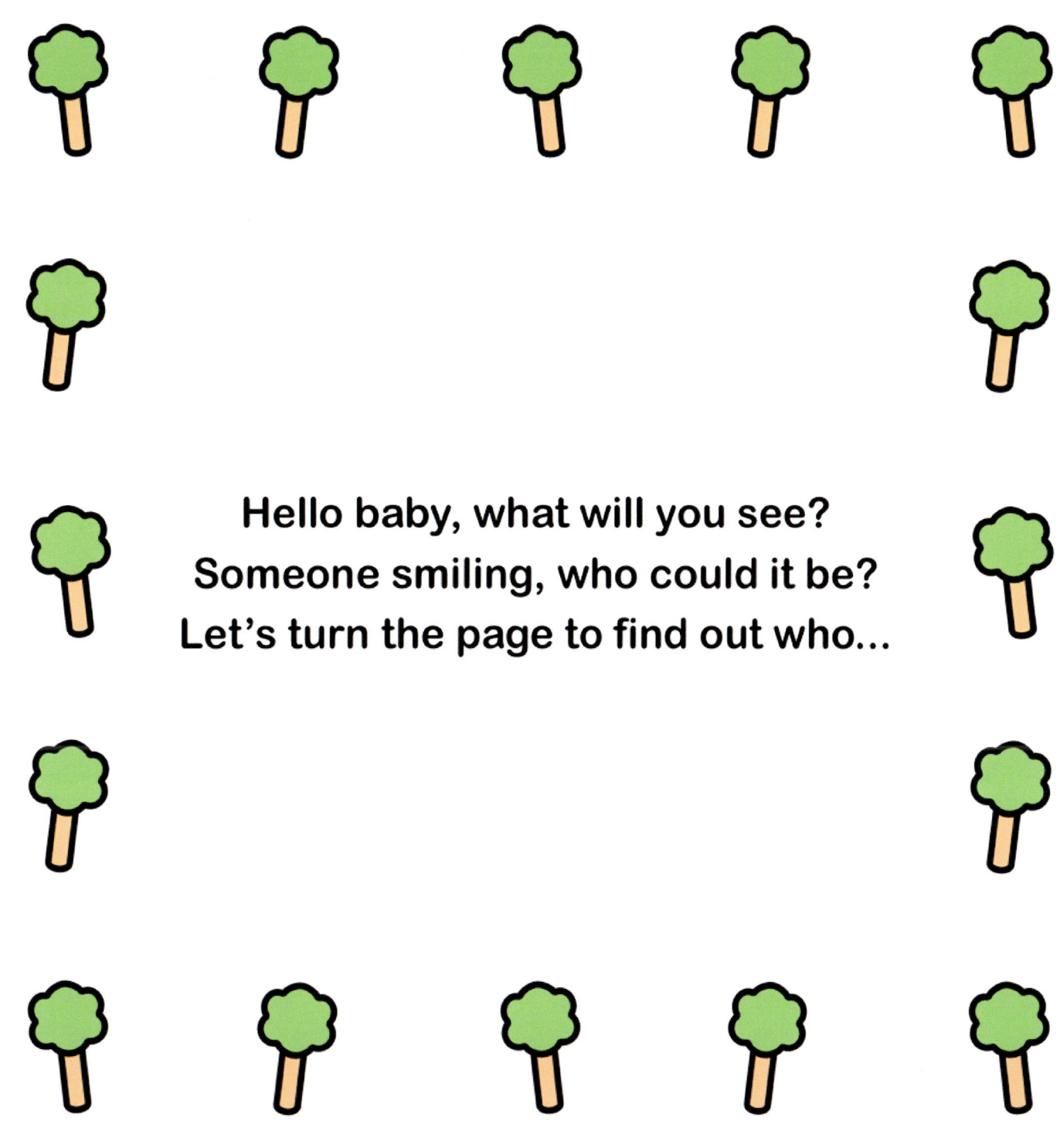

Hello baby, what will you see?
Someone smiling, who could it be?
Let's turn the page to find out who...

It's **grandpa** smiling at you!

Hello baby, what will you see?
Someone smiling, who could it be?
Let's turn the page to find out who…

Hello baby, what will you see?
Someone smiling, who could it be?
Let's turn the page to find out who…

It's **uncle** smiling at you!

Hello baby, what will you see?
Someone smiling, who could it be?
Let's turn the page to find out who…

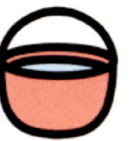

It's the **cousins** smiling at you!

Hello baby, what will you see?
Someone smiling, who could it be?
Let's turn the page to find out who…

It's the **friends** smiling at you!

Hello baby, what will you see?
Someone smiling, who could it be?
Let's turn the page to find out who…

It's the **fur friends** smiling at you!

Hello baby, what will you see?
Someone smiling, who could it be?
Let's turn the page to find out who…

It's **everyone** smiling at you!

Hello baby, what will I see?
Someone smiling, who could it be?
Let's turn the page to find out who…

It's **baby** smiling too!

www.ingramcontent.com/pod-product-compliance
Lightning Source LLC
Chambersburg PA
CBRC092340290426
44109CB00008B/170